The LNER Class D49s
'Hunts' and 'Shires'

Compiled by Alan C Butcher

ISBN 978-1-913893-14-9

First published in 2022 by Transport Treasury Publishing Ltd. 16 Highworth Close, High Wycombe, HP13 7PJ
Totem Publishing, an imprint of Transport Treasury Publishing.

www.ttpublishing.co.uk

Printed in Tarxien, Malta By Gutenberg Press Ltd.

'*The LNER Class D49s*' is one of a series of books on specialist transport subjects published in strictly limited numbers and produced under the Totem Publishing imprint using material only available at The Transport Treasury.

Further reading
Haresnape, Brian, **Gresley Locomotives: A Pictorial History**, Ian Allan Publishing, 978-0-7110-0892-1, 1981.
R.C.T.S., **Locomotives of the LNER: Part 1 – Preliminary Survey**, R.C.T.S., 0-901115-1-8, 1963.
R.C.T.S., **Locomotives of the LNER: Part 4 – Tender Engines**, Classes D25 to E7, (2nd Edn), R.C.T.S., 0-901115-1-0, 1984.
Walmsley, Tony, **Shed by Shed: Part 3 – North Eastern**, St Petroc InfoPublishing, 978-0-9560615-3-9, 2010.
Walmsley, Tony, **Shed by Shed: Part 4 – Scotland**, St Petroc InfoPublishing, 978-0-9560615-7-7, 2011.
Yeadon, W., **Yeadon's Register of LNER Locomotives: Vol 10 Gresley D49& J38 Classes**, ISBN 1-899624-12-0, Challenger Publications, 1996.

Front cover: No 62774 *The Staintondale* is seen on shed at Darlington in 1954. *Neville Stead 206829*
Frontispiece: No 62742 *The Braes of Derwent* is seen awaiting departure from Northallerton in 1954. *Neville Stead 206765*
Rear cover: No 62707 *Lancashire* is seen departing Hull Paragon in 1959. *Neville Stead 208274*

Introduction

At its inception the LNER inherited a considerable number of adequate, but aging 4-4-0s for secondary services. To cater for increased traffic in Scotland, the LNER had built a series of 'Large Directors' to the Great Central Railway design in 1924 for service on the demanding inter-city passenger services. Although liked by the crews, and performing well, when the demand came for additional 4-4-0s, Gresley decided on a new type – his first passenger locomotive design for the LNER. His Pacifics had of course entered service in Great Northern Railway days. The idea being that a modern 4-4-0 could handle not only the local workings but could tackle secondary main line services. The original batch of the D49s, as the three-cylinder 4-4-0s came to be known, were designed with Scotland in mind, although a number were allocated to the North Eastern area. Built at Darlington in 1927/28 this series – named after Scottish and English shire counties – known as D49 Part One [hereafter D49/1], was very much a Gresley design with three cylinders, piston valves and Walschaert's valve gear for the outside cylinders with the inside piston activated by conjugated valve gear. The boilers were pressed at 180psi, normal for the 4-4-0s of the era, which, with 6ft 8in driving wheels gave a tractive effort of 21,555lbs – significantly greater than the pre-grouping locomotives they were designed to supplement or replace.

The class were destined to be the focus of experiments with valve gears. The initial two D49 Part 2 [D49/2] class entered traffic in 1929 fitted with Lentz-patent rotary cam poppet valve gear – designed by Dr Lenz, a South African, the UK licence holder was Davey, Paxman & Co of Colchester. Fifteen locomotives entered service in 1932/33 with an additional 25 in 1934/35. Named after 'Hunts' they were allocated to the LNER's North Eastern Area. Comparative tests with the piston-valved D49/1s showed they were not working economically as the fixed gear ratio of the Lentz gear limited the power range. Apart from one example, No 62764, receiving an infinitely variable gear in BR days no other action was taken.

The six D49/3 'Shires' had the Lentz poppet valves, with oscillating cams, though the primary motion was Walschaert's. This proved problematic for the inside cylinder with over-travel experienced on the valve gear; Gresley's 2 to 1 levers were used in replacement. When the time came for the cylinders to be replaced conventional piston valves were used, and the locomotives reclassified as D49/1.

The only other major change was when Edward Thompson, Gresley's replacement as CME, rebuilt an example – No 365 The Morpeth – as a 'simplified' locomotive featuring two inside-cylinders along the lines of a Great Central Railway 'Director'. It emerged from Darlington with D49/4 lettering on the buffer beam, although officially it was a Class D.

Postwar the Class D49s were relegated to secondary duties by the mixed-traffic Thompson Class B1 4-6-0s at the main sheds. Withdrawal commenced in 1957 (7 members), 30 in 1958, 16 in 1959, 8 in 1960 with the final 14 in 1961. One of the class survives in preservation.

Numbering
When introduced from 1927 the locomotives were given numbers on a seemingly random basis using gaps in the 201-377 series – although the eight locomotives built in 1929 carried Nos 2753-2760. Postwar the LNER was to renumber its locomotive stock in a more logical order, mainly based on the date of entering traffic. The series selected for the 'D49s' was 2700 to 2775; despite eight locomotives already having numbers within this series they were given new ones in construction order. Upon Nationalisation 60000 was added to the number.

Tenders
All 76 locomotives were first coupled with LNER Group Standard tenders, carrying 7.5 tons of coal and 4,200 gallons of water. Two variations were used, stepped topped (used by 43 locomotives) and flush sided (33). 1938 saw the first changes, when the D49/3 rebuilt with piston valves were attached to ex-North Eastern Railway self-trimming tenders from 'Q6' 0-8-0 mineral locomotives carrying 5.5 tons of coal and 4,125 gallons of water. War demands resulted in further changes when Group Standard tenders from some D49s were released for use behind new-build Gresley 'V2' 2-6-2s.

Liveries
As built all were in LNER lined green livery, during World War 2 they lost this in favour of black; with the tender lettering abbreviated to NE. Following the war the full initials were reinstated. Nationalisation saw them in lined black – the new owners name was spelt in Sans Serif lettering on the tender, followed by the first BR lion-over-wheel emblem, then from 1957 the later style when transfers became available – although only 19 tenders were so treated.

Class Data

D49/1: Introduced 1927, Walschaerts valve gear-driven piston valves

D49/2: Introduced 1928, development of D49/1 with Lentz rotary cam poppet valves

D49/3: Locomotives as built 2720-24 with Lentz oscillating valve gear with poppet valves. Between March and September 1938 these were converted to Class D49/1.

D49/4: Introduced 1942, rebuild of D49/2 (No 365) with two inside cylinders of Class D11 pattern

Note: Nos 2751-75 have larger diameter piston valves than the earlier Class D49/1s.

Driving wheel diameter: 6ft 8in
Cylinders (3): 17in x 26in (except rebuilt 2768 [2] 20in x 26in)

Nominal tractive effort: 21,555lb (except rebuilt 2768 19,980lb)

Locomotive weight in working order:
D49/1 – 66 tons
D49/2 – 64 tons 10cwt
D49/4 – 62 tons

Boiler pressure: 180psi

Boiler: barrel length – 11ft 4 5/8 in, firebox external length – 8ft 6in, outside diameter – 5ft 6in

Locomotive weight: 65 tons 11 cwt (total)
Bogie – 23 tons, 11 cwt
Leading driver – 21 ton 5 cwt
Trailing drivers – 20 ton 15 cwt

Route availability: 8

1st No	Name	Class	To Traffic	First Shed	1946 No (date)	BR No (date – w/e)	Withdrawn	Last BR Shed
234	*Yorkshire*	D49/1	29/10/1927	York	2700 (14/04/1946)	62700 (02/04/1949)	08/10/1958	Hull Botanic Gardens

When built the locomotives were not fitted with train heating connections on the front buffer beam; however, a number of the class were retro-fitted from the mid-1930s. No 62700 is seen on shed at Hull Dairycoates in 1958; it was shopped at Darlington between 19 December 1957 and 28 January 1958 following a derailment. It would however be withdrawn a matter of months later. The driver's side front buffer has had a note chalked on advising the shed staff to light the fire! *Neville Stead 206701*

1st No	Name	Class	To Traffic	First Shed	1946 No (date)	BR No (date – w/e)	Withdrawn	Last BR Shed
251	*Derbyshire*	D49/1	26/11/2927	Neville Hill	2701 (01/12/1946)	62701 (12/06/1948)	24/09/195	Hull Dairycoates

Between April 1929 and March 1930 the locomotive was fitted with a Kylala blast pipe for comparison purposes, the advantages were not sufficient for the rest of the class to be so treated and the experiment was terminated after a year. It is here at Hull Botanic Gardens in a somewhat woebegone condition on 23 September 1956 whilst allocated to Bridlington. *Eric Sawford 3986*

1st No	Name	Class	To Traffic	First Shed	1946 No (date)	BR No (date – w/e)	Withdrawn	Last BR Shed
253	*Oxfordshire*	D49/1	30/11/1927	Neville Hill	2702 (12/01/1947)	62702 (01/04/1950)	12/11/1958	Neville Hill

The locomotive was seemingly unlucky in that over the course of a 30-year career it required new cylinders in 1932; it then fractured its main frames in late 1933, receiving a new set in 1937; then having them realigned in the summer of 1946. Perhaps construction was rushed to get it into traffic before the festive season really got under way. Towards the end of their career it was not unusual for members of the class to be put into store during winter months and No 62702 was reported as being in store at York during the winter of 1955/56.

1st No	Name	Class	To Traffic	First Shed	1946 No (date)	BR No (date – w/e)	Withdrawn	Last BR Shed
253	Hertfordshire	D49/1	08/12/1927	Neville Hill	2703 (24/10/1946)	62703 (16/04/1949)	24/06/1958	Hull Botanic Gardens

The locomotive came to an untimely end on 27 May 1958 when it managed to fall into the turntable pit at Bridlington. Towed to Doncaster for assessment it was deemed as being uneconomical to repair and, as the steam era was slowly drawing to a close, it was withdrawn from service and scrapped. Seen at Hull Paragon during 1953, it is attached to an ex-North Eastern Railway tender gained in November 1938. *Neville Stead 206710*

1st No	Name	Class	To Traffic	First Shed	1946 No (date)	BR No (date – w/e)	Withdrawn	Last BR Shed
264	*Stirlingshire*	D49/1	14/12/1927	Haymarket	2704 (09/12/1946)	62704 (17/07/1948)	18/08/1958	Thornton Junction

As built the first deliveries left the works without front steps being fitted – the omission was quickly rectified. This was one of the class fitted with an automatic train control system – developed by Alfred Ernest Hudd in the 1930s – and marketed as the 'Strowger-Hudd' system. World War 2 saw the trials terminated, but the principles were incorporated in to the later BR Automatic Warning System. No 62704 is seen on shed at Thornton Junction on 29 October 1955.

1st No	Name	Class	To Traffic	First Shed	1946 No (date)	BR No (date – w/e)	Withdrawn	Last BR Shed
265	*Lanarkshire*	D49/1	22/12/1927	St Margarets	2705 (09/12/1946)	62705 (15/05/1948)	30/11/1959	Haymarket

Seen at Haymarket depot on 28 April 1957 the locomotive is attached to an ex-Great Central Railway tender that it acquired in January 1942 when its original one was transferred to a new-build Class V2 then under construction to aid the war effort. Initially allocated to St Margarets shed transfer to Haymarket occurred in March 1943 where it stayed for the remainder of its career. Of the locomotives constructed in 1927, No 62705 was in service for 31 years, 11 months and 8 days – recycling occurred at Darlington in January 1960.

1st No	Name	Class	To Traffic	First Shed	1946 No (date)	BR No (date – w/e)	Withdrawn	Last BR Shed
266	*Forfarshire*	D49/1	28/12/1927	Dundee	2706 (22/09/1946)	62706 (04/09/1948)	03/02/1958	Thornton Junction

Like the majority of the D49/1s No 266 exchanged its original tender for a Great Central example, this time in February 1942. The Group Standard tender attached to K3 No 61962 neatly shows the differences between the types. No 266 was transferred to Haymarket in January 1940 before arrival at Thornton Junction in April 1957. Withdrawn in early February 1958, scrapping was carried out the same month at Darlington.

1st No	Name	Class	To Traffic	First Shed	1946 No (date)	BR No (date – w/e)	Withdrawn	Last BR Shed
236	*Lancashire*	D49/1	14/01/2028	Neville Hill	2707 (12/05/1946)	62707 (29/05/1947)	06/10/1959	Hull Dairycoates

All lines had a route availability rating that indicated the maximum axle loading possible. The D49s with a weight of 21 tons 5cwt on the leading axle were RA8, virtually limiting them to the main lines. This limit is indicated with the rating painted onto the lower cab side plating. No 62707 spent its BR career shuttling between Bridlington and Hull depots; it is seen at Hull Botanic Gardens in 1959. *Neville Stead 208001*

1st No	Name	Class	To Traffic	First Shed	1946 No (date)	BR No (date – w/e)	Withdrawn	Last BR Shed
270	*Argyllshire*	D49/1	20/01/1928	Haymarket	2708 (14/09/1946)	62708 (01/04/1950)	04/05/1959	Thornton Junction

The first 28 locomotives were fitted with dual – air and vacuum – brakes; the Westinghouse pump for operating the air-braked carriages on the North Eastern and Scottish Areas is shown fitted to the fireman's side. By the 1930s the Areas had sufficient vacuum-braked carriages for the air-braking system to be removed. The locomotive was allocated to Haymarket, where it is seen in 1929, until January 1935 when it was transferred to Dundee, spending the next eight years there.

1st No	Name	Class	To Traffic	First Shed	1946 No (date)	BR No (date – w/e)	Withdrawn	Last BR Shed
277	*Berwickshire*	D49/1	24/01/1928	St Margarets	2709 (07/09/1946)	62709 (01/04/1950)	01/01/1960	Haymarket

When the D49/2s were constructed five boilers were built by Robert Stephenson at its Darlington Works – just across the road from the LNER's facilities. These boilers can be identified by the four washout plugs above the firebox on each side as were the 10 constructed by Cowlairs Works. With boiler changes taking place throughout the history of the class the 15 four washout plug boilers were fitted to other members as seen here – a potential trap for modellers. It was allocated to Haymarket in March 1943, where it is seen, and throughout its subsequent career.

1st No	Name	Class	To Traffic	First Shed	1946 No (date)	BR No (date – w/e)	Withdrawn	Last BR Shed
245	*Lincolnshire*	D49/1	07/02/1928	Neville Hill	2710 (14/09/1946)	62710 (19/10/1948)	03/10/1960	Hull Dairycoates

The locomotive was, unusually, allocated to Kings Cross for a few months – September 1928 to April 1929. Ex-works on 23 January 1948 this was the last D49 to have the former owner's initials – LNER – on the tender; the new owners name then appeared on ex-works locomotives. It is seen at Darlington Works, by now carrying the first BR emblem, awaiting its return to Hull Botanic Gardens where it was allocated to in January 1955. *Neville Stead 206719*

1st No	Name	Class	To Traffic	First Shed	1946 No (date)	BR No (date – w/e)	Withdrawn	Last BR Shed
281	*Dumbartonshire*	D49/1	09/02/1928	St Margarets	2711 (14/09/1946)	62711 (23/10/1948)	01/05/1961	Harwick

In 1948/49 Darlington found it necessary to rebody 10 ex-Great Central Railway tenders coupled to the D49s. The frames and wheels were retained, but a flush-sided tank was put on with the coping moved from a central to a more forward position. Water capacity on the rebuild dropped from 4,000 to 3,800 gallons.
No 62711 is seen on 10 September 1960 sporting the incorrect spelling on the nameplate – the county name is Dunbartonshire. It was disposed of at Darlington in June 1961.

1st No	Name	Class	To Traffic	First Shed	1946 No (date)	BR No (date – w/e)	Withdrawn	Last BR Shed
246	*Morayshire*	D49/1	20/02/1928	Dundee	2712 (10/11/1946)	62712 (01/04/1950)	03/07/1961	Harwick

Condemned in July 1961 No 62712 was sent to Slateford Laundry in Edinburgh to serve as a stationary boiler until January 1962. It spent the next 30 months in store; seemingly forgotten, it evaded being called to Darlington for recycling resulting in its sale for preservation in July 1964. The mark by the number was a hole, through the cab side, that was occupied by the control rod for the tablet collecting apparatus fitted to locomotives operating over the single-track section between Dundee and Aberdeen. When the apparatus was removed Cowlairs generally plugged the hole – although *Morayshire* retained the hole into preservation.

1st No	Name	Class	To Traffic	First Shed	1946 No (date)	BR No (date – w/e)	Withdrawn	Last BR Shed
249	*Aberdeenshire*	D49/1	21/02/1928	Dundee	2713 (14/09/1946)	62713 (03/07/1948)	09/09/1957	Thornton Junction

One of the least travelled locomotives, No 62713 was only ever allocated to two depots – Dundee and Thornton Junction. Seen here attached to a Group Standard tender, sometime between receiving a Great Central Railway example, in December 1942, and a North Eastern example in August 1957 that it took to the scrapyard a month later as the first member of the D49/1s to be withdrawn. Scrapping occurred at Darlington in October the same year.

1st No	Name	Class	To Traffic	First Shed	1946 No (date)	BR No (date – w/e)	Withdrawn	Last BR Shed
250	*Perthshire*	D49/1	02/03/1928	Perth	2714 (10/11/1946)	62714 (15/10/1949)	26/08/1959	Stirling

The tender was one of four Great Central replacements, with the coal rails plated on the inside to stop small lumps falling out. Gresley's A3 Pacific No 60035 *Windsor Lad* can be seen to the right of the image emerging from the shed at Haymarket on 5 November 1955 from where it was withdrawn on 4 September 1961. No 62714 was initially allocated to Perth before making its one and only transfer to Stirling on 9 September 1951. Disposal occurred at Darlington two months after withdrawal.

1st No	Name	Class	To Traffic	First Shed	1946 No (date)	BR No (date – w/e)	Withdrawn	Last BR Shed
306	*Roxburghshire*	D49/1	06/03/1928	St Margarets	2715 (17/11/1946)	62715 (05/02/1949)	29/06/1959	St Margarets

One feature of Darlington-designed locomotives was the positioning of the top lamp iron on the smokebox in front of the chimney. In Scotland the position was amended to the top of the smokebox door when the class went to Cowlairs Works for maintenance. Scottish area locomotives were fitted with a pair of clips on the ring of the smokebox door to hold a destination board that can be seen on No 329 (page 30). However, by nationalisation the Darlington custom had prevailed and thereafter the lamp irons were restored to the top of the smokebox.

1st No	Name	Class	To Traffic	First Shed	1946 No (date)	BR No (date – w/e)	Withdrawn	Last BR Shed
307	*Kincardineshire*	D49/1	17/03/1928	Dundee	2716 (27/10/1946)	62716 (01/04/1950)	28/04/1961	St Margarets

The tender carries its new owner title in full on the tender in 10in Sans Serif lettering; however, five examples – Nos 62705, 62724, 62749, 62762 and 62769 – sported 8in lettering. From 23 August 1949 Darlington ceased applying the lettering because all locomotives were to carry the lion-over-wheel emblem. The inside-plated tender, acquired in June 1942, was the last in service. No 62716 is seen at Thornton Junction on 16 March 1952.

1st No	Name	Class	To Traffic	First Shed	1946 No (date)	BR No (date – w/e)	Withdrawn	Last BR Shed
309	*Banffshire*	D49/1	26/03/192	Dundee	2717 (09/12/1946)	62717 (30/09/1950)	13/01/1961	Hull Dairycoates

Locomotives built up to August 1933 and allocated to the North Eastern Area – six D49/1s, 17 D49/2s and five D49/3s – and five allocated to the Scottish Area – Nos 264, 270, 309, 329 and 2754 – were fitted with Raven fog signalling apparatus. The plunger was fitted beneath the cab. At the end of October 1933 the system went out of use. The fireman, standing on the tender, will be trimming the coal as it may well foul the loading gauge while the driver ensues the water column valve is turned off at Eastfield on 15 April 1948. No 2717 would retain its LNER number for another two years. During its 32 year career No 62717 is recorded as covering over 1.2 million miles.

1st No	Name	Class	To Traffic	First Shed	1946 No (date)	BR No (date – w/e)	Withdrawn	Last BR Shed
310	*Kinross-shire*	D49/1	03/05/1928	Dundee	2718 (08/12/1946)	62718 (15/01/1949)	24/04/1961	St Margarets

Before the introduction of the 60000 number series some locomotives had the 'owning' regions initial place before the number, as demonstrated by E2718 that received it on 19 March 1948. Only another four members of the class – 2713, 2736, 2770 and 2773 – were so adorned. The tender still carries the former owner's full initials. On the left hand side of the smokebox was a circular cover that covered the superheater header end.

1st No	Name	Class	To Traffic	First Shed	1946 No (date)	BR No (date – w/e)	Withdrawn	Last BR Shed
311	*Peebles-shire*	D49/1	05/05/1928	St Margarets	2719 (14/09/1946)	62719 (12/03/1949)	01/01/1960	Harwick

The depot's coaling tower and water tank loom over the locomotive at Haymarket on 9 March 1952. Coded 64B by BR the depot was home shed to only six members of the class during the BR era. The depot was home for No 62719 from March 1943 to November 1959 when it was transferred to Harwick; withdrawal came a couple of months later and it was swiftly disposed of at Darlington.

1st No	Name	Class	To Traffic	First Shed	1946 No (date)	BR No (date – w/e)	Withdrawn	Last BR Shed
318	*Cambridgeshire*	D49/3	07/05/1928	Neville Hill	2720 (01/12/1946)	62720 (07/05/1949)	06/10/1959	Hull Dairycoates

The tender fitted to the locomotive at the time of the photograph, an ex-North Eastern Railway 'Q6' one, was unique in that the coal rails had been cut off square at the rear rather than the usual dipped style. Remarkably clean when photographed at Darlington the locomotive was probably just ex works, having had a non-classified overhaul between 12-19 May 1949. This was the first of the Class 49/3 variants fitted with Lentz oscillating valve gear with poppet valves. Between March and September 1938 these were converted to Class D49/1 specification; No 318 was converted at Darlington in spring 1938.
Neville Stead 206730

1st No	Name	Class	To Traffic	First Shed	1946 No (date)	BR No (date – w/e)	Withdrawn	Last BR Shed
320	*Warwickshire*	D49/3	23/05/1928	York	2721 (08/12/1946)	62721 (26/03/1949)	18/08/1958	St Margarets

Having been constructed as a D49/3 the locomotive was converted to Class 49/1 specification at Darlington in spring 1938 when it was fitted with piston valves. It was reported in March 1949 that the locomotive was ex-works at Darlington following a General overhaul – having arrived on 31 January it was released to traffic on 19 March. Its original Group Standard tender was replaced by a North Eastern one in March 1938 with the Great Central version shown here being acquired in April 1944.

1st No	Name	Class	To Traffic	First Shed	1946 No (date)	BR No (date – w/e)	Withdrawn	Last BR Shed
322	*Huntingdonshire*	D49/3	10/07/1928	York	2722 (12/11/1946)	62722 (29/05/1948)	20/10/1959	Hull Dairycoates

Like its class mates, No 322 was converted to Class 49/1 specification at Darlington in autumn 1938. It spent 27 years allocated to Hull Botanic Gardens, from May 1932 until June 1959, where it is seen a few months before departure to the neighbouring Dairycoates depot when Botanic Gardens closed to steam. Unless the tender emblem is hidden under a coat of grime it appears to be missing – although as the cab side number is also barely visible the locomotive is in need of a clean! *Neville Stead 208002*

1st No	Name	Class	To Traffic	First Shed	1946 No (date)	BR No (date – w/e)	Withdrawn	Last BR Shed
327	*Nottinghamshire*	D49/3	11/07/1928	York	2723 (30/11/1946)	62723 (16/10/1948)	16/01/1961	Hull Dairycoates

No 327 was converted to Class 49/1 at Darlington in early summer 1938; it was the last of the conversions to be scrapped at Darlington in 1961. It is seen at Hull Botanic Gardens with the BR emblem on the tender looking as if cleaning has recently revealed it. Transfers for the 1956-design crest were not available until 1957 so the locomotive probably acquired the new version during a general repair at Darlington during the summer of 1957.
Neville Stead 206687

1st No	Name	Class	To Traffic	First Shed	1946 No (date)	BR No (date – w/e)	Withdrawn	Last BR Shed
335	*Bedfordshire*	D49/3	28/08/1928	York	2724 (12/12/1946)	62724 (29/05/1948)	17/12/1957	Hull Botanic Gardens

As No 335 it was the first class member to have the number on the cab side and the only one to be fitted with a M. L. S. (Marine, Locomotive and Stationary) superheater and multiple valve regulator resulting in the control rod being on the right (fireman's side) of the boiler. Converted to Class 49/1 specification at Darlington in autumn 1938 it acquired the North Eastern Railway tender seen here when it was photographed on Darlington depot during 1947.
Neville Stead 206737

1st No	Name	Class	To Traffic	First Shed	1946 No (date)	BR No (date – w/e)	Withdrawn	Last BR Shed
329	*Inverness-shire*	D49/3	30/08/1928	Perth	2725 (15/12/1946)	62725 (01/01/1950)	10/11/1958	Stirling (South)

The final D49/3 variant was also the last new locomotive to enter traffic with the number displayed on the tender. The drive to the poppet valves needed improvement in June 1929 and it left the works with the number transferred to the cab side. Further alterations occurred when it was converted to Class 49/1 specification at Darlington in autumn 1938. The locomotive spent three periods allocated to Perth and three at York before settling in Scotland from April 1938.

1st No	Name	Class	To Traffic	First Shed	1946 No (date)	BR No (date – w/e)	Withdrawn	Last BR Shed
352	*Leicestershire*	D49/2	15/03/1929	York	–	–	Renamed	–
352	*The Meynell*	D49/2	08/06/1932	–	2726 (01/12/1946)	62726 (18/06/1949)	18/12/1957	Scarborough

The last two locomotives of the 1926 order did not enter traffic until 1929 and, fitted with Lentz poppet valve gear, initiated the D49/2 variation. In 1932 when the decision was taken that all the D49/2 variants were to be named after Hunts, resulting in the need to rename them from 'Shires' to a 'Hunt's. The change of nameplate took place at Darlington after a non-classified visit to Darlington Works between 30 May and 7 June 1932. It is seen with its new name inside an otherwise empty York North shed where it was allocated at the time.

1st No	Name	Class	To Traffic	First Shed	1946 No (date)	BR No (date – w/e)	Withdrawn	Last BR Shed
336	*Buckinghamshire*	D49/2	01/06/1929	York	–	–	Renamed	–
336	*The Quorn*	D49/2	09/05/1932	–	2727 (17/11/1946)	62727 (19/08/1950)	16/01/1961	Hull Dairycoates

The second locomotive to be renamed, No 336, is seen here in both guises. The change of nameplate took place at Darlington during a general overhaul at the works between 3 March and 9 May 1932. No 62727 is seen at Starbeck on 1 August 1955. All locomotives built prior to May 1932, and Nos 201 and 211, had cylinder drainpipes that terminated by the rim of the leading wheel of the bogie (see inset). Initially on the D49/2s the operating linkage for the drain cocks was to the rear of the cylinders, they were gradually changed to reflect the arrangement used on the D49/1s.

1st No	Name	Class	To Traffic	First Shed	1946 No (date)	BR No (date – w/e)	Withdrawn	Last BR Shed
2753	Cheshire	D49/1	20/02/1929	Eastfield	2728 (07/04/1946)	62728 (15/05/1948)	29/10/1959	Thornton Junction

When new the D49s were fitted with steam-operated reversing gear. However, the Scottish footplate crews did not find it any advantage and within a matter of months the locomotives had been modified to the more traditional screw-operated version. The original 2753 to 2760 batch differed from previous builds in having screw-reversing gear fitted from new. Always a Scottish Region locomotive No 62728 was called south to Darlington Works in October 1959, it is seen at Whessoe Lane Yard, Darlington, shortly before being condemned. *Neville Stead 208515*

1st No	Name	Class	To Traffic	First Shed	1946 No (date)	BR No (date – w/e)	Withdrawn	Last BR Shed
2754	*Rutlandshire*	D49/1	08/04/1929	Eastfield	2729 (13/07/1946)	62729 (11/09/1948)	01/05/1961	St Margarets

Only the D49/2 and D49/3 variants were fitted with outside steam pipes, but this D49/1 has acquired a smokebox saddle from one of them as shown by the gap in its top edge. When the locomotive was shopped at Darlington Works in November 1957 three of the D49/2s had reached the end of their lives and one donated its saddle to replace that originally fitted. Following its return to Scotland it is seen at Thornton Junction shed in 1959. *Neville Stead 208452*

1st No	Name	Class	To Traffic	First Shed	1946 No (date)	BR No (date – w/e)	Withdrawn	Last BR Shed
2755	*Berkshire*	D49/1	15/03/1929	Eastfield	2730 (02/06/1946)	62730 (02/10/1948)	11/12/1958	Selby

In June 1927 Gresley issued a list of 28 county names to Darlington asking for a nameplate design to be produced. The initial selection was divided into two groups – 13 English county names for use on North Eastern Area locomotives and 15 Scottish Area ones; these were for counties that the LNER directly served or ran services to. The next batch included Berkshire, which was not served by the LNER, but others such as County Durham – where Darlington is actually located – were not. With Windsor Castle in Berkshire maybe Gresley was looking for a knighthood!

1st No	Name	Class	To Traffic	First Shed	1946 No (date)	BR No (date – w/e)	Withdrawn	Last BR Shed
2756	*Selkirkshire*	D49/1	21/03/1929	Eastfield	2731 (02/06/1946)	62731 (19/09/1948)	03/04/1959	Selby

A fairly nomadic locomotive it was delivered to Eastfield shed, Glasgow, when new then transferred to Carlisle. It spent it BR career shuttling round the North Eastern Area, including three periods at York. Confusingly it was one of eight locomotives to carry original numbers – 2753-60 – that were to be changed for others in the same series – 2728-2735 – under the 1946 renumbering scheme. When photographed it was still paired with its Group Standard tender, replacement came in July 1942 in the shape of an ex-Great Central Railway design, its original going to a new-build Class O2 2-8-0.

1st No	Name	Class	To Traffic	First Shed	1946 No (date)	BR No (date – w/e)	Withdrawn	Last BR Shed
2757	*Dumfries-shire*	D49/1	28/03/1929	Eastfield	2732 (12/04/1946)	62732 (19/09/1948)	03/11/1958	Darlington

All locomotives were fitted for applying sand by gravity to the front leading coupled wheels. In Scotland it was found necessary to add rear sanding to the trailing drivers for reversing up Cowlairs incline after working into Glasgow (Queen Street). From March 1933 Cowlairs added rear sanding to 15 D49/1s allocated to Eastfield, Haymarket and St Margarets – Nos 264, 265, 270, 277, 281, 306, 311 and 2753-60. No other locomotives were fitted for another 10 years, but between September 1943 and October 1946, when the whole class had at least one heavy repair at Cowlairs, three D49/1s and 14 D49/2s were so fitted whilst they were there for attention. No 62732 is seen at Haymarket on 22 February 1953.

1st No	Name	Class	To Traffic	First Shed	1946 No (date)	BR No (date – w/e)	Withdrawn	Last BR Shed
2758	*Northumberland*	D49/1	28/03/1929	Eastfield	2733 (01/12/1946)	62733 (10/04/1948)	24/04/1961	Harwick

This was one of the class fitted with Hudd automatic train control in June 1939 until it was removed in February 1943. The BR number has been newly painted with 10-inch numerals, although the tender retains its austerity NE lettering that first appeared in July 1942. The locomotive received its new identity in April 1948 whilst shedded at Haymarket between August 1943 and January 1958 where it is seen.

1st No	Name	Class	To Traffic	First Shed	1946 No (date)	BR No (date – w/e)	Withdrawn	Last BR Shed
2759	*Cumberland*	D49/1	31/05/1929	Eastfield	2374 (17/11/1946)	62734 (19/09/1948)	04/03/1961	Carlisle Canal

A variation on the number size – this time in 8 inch numerals, and not so skilfully applied and appearing to have been painted on to an uncleaned cab side. It is seen at Haymarket on 22 May 1949 having worked in from Carlisle Canal depot where it was allocated for two periods – December 1946 – September 1950 and from July 1951 until withdrawal. Called to Darlington in March 1961 it was withdrawn, having a service life of 32 years 27 days.

1st No	Name	Class	To Traffic	First Shed	1946 No (date)	BR No (date – w/e)	Withdrawn	Last BR Shed
2760	*Westmorland*	D49/1	20/06/1929	Eastfield	2735 (17/11/1746)	62735 (19/09/1948)	25/08/1958	Scarborough

Westmorland is seen at York where it was allocated between October 1950 and April 1954. It was reported to be one of nine members of the class in storage at Whitby in October 1957; it would be resurrected for a final fling before withdrawal from Scarborough depot the following year. Summoned to Darlington in August 1958 it was withdrawn and scrapped in November. *Neville Stead 206756*

1st No	Name	Class	To Traffic	First Shed	1946 No (date)	BR No (date – w/e)	Withdrawn	Last BR Shed
201	*The Bramham Moor*	D49/2	20/04/1932	Neville Hill	2736 (14/04/1946)	62736 (04/10/1950)	19/06/1958	Starbeck

The Class D49/2s were fitted with Lentz rotary cam poppet valves with the introduction of 'Hunt' names. These were also fitted with rocking grates and hinged glass sight screen cab sides from new; these items were retro-fitted to earlier locomotives as they went through the works. The locomotive is seen on shed at Starbeck in 1955 having arrived there from York (North) in October 1950. *Neville Stead 206758*

1st No	Name	Class	To Traffic	First Shed	1946 No (date)	BR No (date – w/e)	Withdrawn	Last BR Shed
211	*The York and Ainsty*	D49/2	04/05/1932	Neville Hill	2737 (28/04/1946)	62737 (08/05/1948)	01/01/1958	Hull Botanic Gardens

No 62737 is seen in the Scarborough carriage sidings on 31 July 1955, whilst allocated to Hull Botanic Gardens; arriving at Hull in May 1946 it stayed there throughout its BR career. The lion-over-wheel emblem on the step-sided tender can barely be seen on the original print. The 'Hunt' nameplate was surmounted by a running fox, these were handed so it was always facing forwards. An early withdrawal, it was one of four of the class recycled at Darlington in February 1958.

1st No	Name	Class	To Traffic	First Shed	1946 No (date)	BR No (date – w/e)	Withdrawn	Last BR Shed
220	*The Zetland*	D49/2	03/05/1932	Neville Hill	2738 (19/05/1946)	62738 (12/02/1949)	21/09/1959	York

Between August 1949 and May 1952 five locomotives – Nos 62738/41/42/43/44 – had their solid bronze axle boxes changed to cast steel with manganese steel liners to the horn checks. To feed the new axle boxes an additional 4-feed Wakefield mechanical lubricator was fitted to the left hand running plate (immediately to the front of the splasher). Allocated to Starbeck when that depot closed on 13 September 1959 the locomotive was reallocated to York, although this might have been a 'paper' transfer as withdrawal occurred just eight days later.

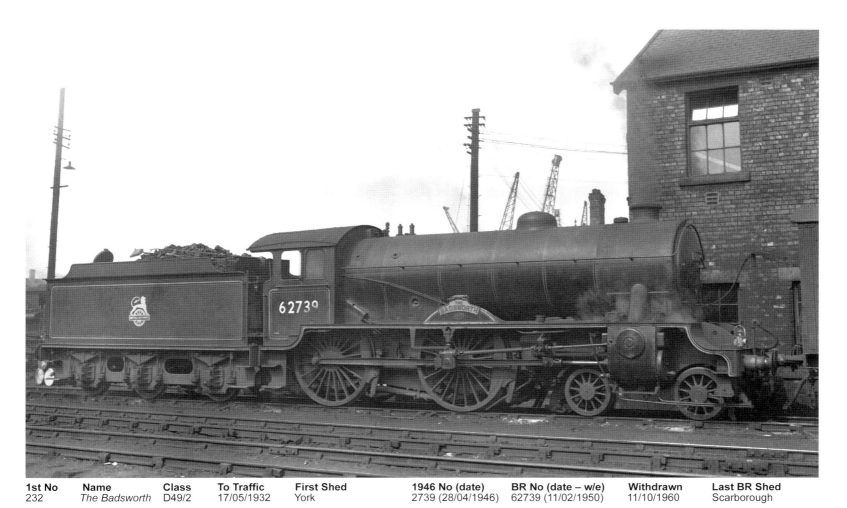

1st No	Name	Class	To Traffic	First Shed	1946 No (date)	BR No (date – w/e)	Withdrawn	Last BR Shed
232	*The Badsworth*	D49/2	17/05/1932	York	2739 (28/04/1946)	62739 (11/02/1950)	11/10/1960	Scarborough

With early withdrawal planned for the class, visits to the Darlington paint shop ceased in June 1958 – only eleven D49/1s and eight D49/2s received the 1956 crest. No 62739 was to receive the new one during a General overhaul between 3 April and 8 May 1958. No 62739 is seen at Middlesbrough on 17 June 1952. Called into Darlington Works in October 1960, the decision was to withdraw the locomotive, one of three taken out of service that month; dismantling occurred within a matter of days.

1st No	Name	Class	To Traffic	First Shed	1946 No (date)	BR No (date – w/e)	Withdrawn	Last BR Shed
235	*The Bedale*	D49/2	02/06/1932	York	2740 (28/04/1946)	62740 (03/12/1949)	01/08/1960	Hull Dairycoates

The standard LNER livery applied by Darlington Works included painting the cylinder cladding in lined green as seen on a clean No 205. Perhaps of more interest alongside is the experimental Kitson-Still steam/diesel hybrid locomotive. It ran most of its trials on LNER lines, and regularly ran a daily freight service from York in 1933-4. The basic principle was that of a diesel engine with double acting pistons. One side of the pistons was diesel, and the other side was operated by steam. The engine was started by steam, and when sufficient speed was reached, diesel fuel was injected into the diesel side of the cylinders. Development and testing of the Kitson-Still engine took the good part of ten years and at great expense. As such, it was a large contributing factor to the downfall of Kitson & Co, who called in the receivers in 1934. After this, the engine was laid up at York North Shed until at least July 1935, after which it returned to Kitsons to be disposed of.

1st No	Name	Class	To Traffic	First Shed	1946 No (date)	BR No (date – w/e)	Withdrawn	Last BR Shed
247	*The Blankney*	D49/2	14/07/1932	Hull Dairycoates	2741 (08/09/1946)	62741 (27/08/1949)	30/10/1958	Hull Botanic Gardens

When new all locomotives were fitted with a slightly dished smokebox door and an outer rim with a flat flange as seen here on No 247 at Scarborough. After 1943 when the front or smokebox door required replacement a modified design was used. That was more dished with no flat flange, but sealed by a pressed joint ring; the image pre-dates the fitting of a steam heat connection on the front buffer beam that occurred during a general overhaul in September/October 1937. The 'Scarborough Flyer' ran from London Kings Cross between 1927 and 1963 – the 'D49' would have taken over the service at York.

1st No	Name	Class	To Traffic	First Shed	1946 No (date)	BR No (date – w/e)	Withdrawn	Last BR Shed
255	*The Braes of Derwent*	D49/2	03/08/1932	York	2742 (27/10/1946)	62742 (03/09/1949)	12/11/1958	Neville Hill

The locomotive leads a rake of cattle vans through York station on 22 May 1950. Note the BR number on the buffer beam as the smokebox number plate has yet to be fitted; the tender retains its austerity NE lettering. With livestock on board the train carries a Class A head code (lamps over buffers) rather than the more usual Class C (headlamps over right hand buffer and coupling). Transferred to Neville Hill in October 1950 it would remain there until withdrawal in 1958.

1st No	Name	Class	To Traffic	First Shed	1946 No (date)	BR No (date – w/e)	Withdrawn	Last BR Shed
269	*The Cleveland*	D49/2	23/08/1932	York	2743 (17/11/1946)	62743 (15/10/1948)	09/05/1960	Haymarket

The Cleveland arrived in Scotland from Hull Botanic Gardens depot in January 1951, remaining at Haymarket until withdrawal. Called to Darlington works in April 1960 repairs were not authorised and it was withdrawn the following month. Note the additional four-feed Wakefield mechanical lubricator fitted to the left hand running plate acquired during a general repair at Darlington between 24 August and 15 December 1950.

1st No	Name	Class	To Traffic	First Shed	1946 No (date)	BR No (date – w/e)	Withdrawn	Last BR Shed
273	*The Holderness*	D49/2	12/10/1932	Neville Hill	2744 (15/12/1946)	62744 (15/10/1948)	30/12/1960	Harwick

The only 'Hunt' to be allocated to Dundee Tay Bridge depot was No 62744, arriving from York in March 1952 it moved to Thornton Junction in February 1957. It was photographed in the shed yard on 20 September 1954. Assigned to Cowlairs for repairs in December 1960 it was not repaired and, unusually was scrapped at the Works. Unlike Darlington where the end was swift, the Scots were slightly slower, with cutting the tender not commencing until 20 February and the locomotive on 14 March 1962.

1st No	Name	Class	To Traffic	First Shed	1946 No (date)	BR No (date – w/e)	Withdrawn	Last BR Shed
282	*The Hurworth*	D49/2	24/10/1932	Neville Hill	2745 (27/10/1946)	62745 (14/05/1949)	16/03/1959	Scarborough

It was reported that on Sunday, 23 January 1955, the annual D'Oyly Carte Opera special from Harrogate (via Leeds) arrived at York at 11.30am behind No 62745, with three London Midland Region passenger carriages and three scenery vans. Allocated to Starbeck at the time, No 62745 was transferred to York in June that year. A move to Scarborough followed in August 1958; called to Darlington in March 1959 it was condemned having a service life of 26 years, 4 months and 20 days.

1st No	Name	Class	To Traffic	First Shed	1946 No (date)	BR No (date – w/e)	Withdrawn	Last BR Shed
283	*The Middleton*	D49/2	18/08/1933	York	2746 (10/11/1946)	62746 (01/05/1948)	04/05/1958	Starbeck

This was the only locomotive fitted with Smith speed indicating equipment when new, it lasted only a matter of months certainly having been removed by the following September. It is seen here at Starbeck on 1 August 1955 in the company of ex-North Eastern Railway Class J25 0-6-0 No 65673 – that had a life of just over 59 years; by comparison No 62746 survived for 24 years 8 months and 28 days.

1st No	Name	Class	To Traffic	First Shed	1946 No (date)	BR No (date – w/e)	Withdrawn	Last BR Shed
288	*The Percy*	D49/2	21/08/1933	York	2747 (08/12/1946)	62747 (24/04/1948)	04/03/1961	Carlisle Canal

The storage of locomotives during the 'off' seasons was not unknown and chimney coverings were used to keep the rain out of the smokebox. Towards the end of steam the sight became more common, *The Percy* is seen in store at Baileyfield in the company of a classmate. The locomotive was fitted with new cylinders at Darlington during a light casual repair between September 1957 and January 1958 only a few months after having a general overhaul – this fact possibly saved it from an early withdrawal as the scrapping of the class had commenced in December 1957.

1st No	Name	Class	To Traffic	First Shed	1946 No (date)	BR No (date – w/e)	Withdrawn	Last BR Shed
292	*The Southwold*	D49/2	23/08/1933	Hull Botanic Gardens	2748 (12/01/1947)	62748 (11/06/1949)	17/12/1957	Neville Hill

The Southwold is seen here at the head of an express service at York, on 19 May 1952, the poster on the right advertises the delights of Essex. It was reported that one of the excursion trains, between Leeds City and Wetherby Racecourse station, on Easter Monday (19 April 1954) was headed by No 62748. No 62748 spent it entire BR career allocated to Neville Hill. Condemned in December 1957 it was cut up the following month.

1st No	Name	Class	To Traffic	First Shed	1946 No (date)	BR No (date – w/e)	Withdrawn	Last BR Shed
297	*The Cottesmore*	D49/2	30/08/1933	York	2749 (14/07/1946)	62749 (01/05/1948)	02/07/1958	Neville Hill

No 297 carries one of the four washout plugs per side boilers that were fitted to the 15 'Hunt' locomotives built in 1923/33. The locomotive, seen here at Darlington, carried this boiler until a general overhaul in April 1937; a light overhaul between 8 September and 18 October 1937 saw the fitting of a steam heat connection, conveniently dating the photograph to that time frame.

1st No	Name	Class	To Traffic	First Shed	1946 No (date)	BR No (date – w/e)	Withdrawn	Last BR Shed
298	*The Pytchley*	D49/2	01/09/1933	York	2750 (01/12/1946)	62750 (29/10/1949)	04/11/1958	Hull Botanic Gardens

No 62750 was allocated at Bridlington from September 1955 until the depot closed on 16th September with the entire allocation being transferred to Hull Botanic Gardens. The end is nigh as the locomotive stands in store at Darlington late in 1958 following withdrawal, recycling occurred during January 1959. In 1987 the model manufacturer Hornby introduced a model of this locomotive (reference R860) in the condition seen here – albeit with Walschaerts valve gear! *Neville Stead 206775*

1st No	Name	Class	To Traffic	First Shed	1946 No (date)	BR No (date – w/e)	Withdrawn	Last BR Shed
205	*The Albrighton*	D49/2	10/07/1934	Hull Botanic Gardens	2751 (02/06/1946)	62751 (10/06/1948)	13/03/1959	Scarborough

As built all locomotives had the fall plate covering the gap – between locomotive and tender – hinged on the tender to ride free on the footplate. Experience showed that the arrangement could lead to occasional cases of a fireman having a foot trapped. From around 1940 this hazard was reduced by hinging the fall plate so as to ride free on the tender. This put the danger area further to the rear – all locomotives were changed irrespective of the type of tender used. In the case of No 62751 this may have occurred at Darlington between 15-23 June 1948 when the tender received attention at Darlington.

1st No	Name	Class	To Traffic	First Shed	1946 No (date)	BR No (date – w/e)	Withdrawn	Last BR Shed
214	*The Atherstone*	D49/2	14/07/1934	Hull Botanic Gardens	2752 (31/03/1946)	62752 (17/04/1948)	29/07/1958	Starbeck

In December 1937 Darlington specially painted the locomotive with 'Syntholux' to see if the additional cost could be justified by its durability – there was little improvement compared with the usual paint used; however, Syntholux paint is still available although not generally used on steam locomotives. The location is Starbeck depot where the locomotive spent the duration of its BR career. It was reported that during mid-October 1955 was observed working a morning Sunderland-Newcastle slow passenger train as a running-in turn following a non-classified overhaul at Darlington. *Neville Stead 206781*

1st No	Name	Class	To Traffic	First Shed	1946 No (date)	BR No (date – w/e)	Withdrawn	Last BR Shed
217	*The Belvoir*	D49/2	17/07/1934	Neville Hill	2753 (28/04/1946)	62753 (16/04/1948)	22/09/1959	York

No 2753 was in Gateshead Works for light repairs when the renumbering to the 60000-series commenced, leaving the works with its new identity painted on the cab sides, although the tender retained its LNER lettering. One of several D49s to be at Starbeck depot when closure took place – 13 September 1959 – No 62753 was transferred to York only to be withdrawn nine days later. It is seen here in better times, albeit in careworn condition, at York on 4 August 1956.

1st No	Name	Class	To Traffic	First Shed	1946 No (date)	BR No (date – w/e)	Withdraw	Last BR Shed
222	*The Berkeley*	D49/2	20/07/1934	Scarborough	2754 (12/10/1946)	62754 (08/01/1949)	03/11/1958	Hull Botanic Gardens

Having gained its BR number at a general overhaul in January 1949, and sporting the first BR lion-over-wheel emblem, it is seen at Hull on Sunday 15 June 1952. One of the Sunday jobs at most depots would be shunting locomotives into position for the following days services; No 62754 is seen here shunting Class K3 2-6-0 No 61813. Prior to disposal, at Darlington during February 1959, No 62754 was stored at North Road station in the company of three Class A5 and two Class A8 Pacific tanks all destined for the Darlington scrap yard.

1st No	Name	Class	To Traffic	First Shed	1946 No (date)	BR No (date – w/e)	Withdrawn	Last BR Shed
226	*The Bilsdale*	D49/2	23/07/1934	Scarborough	2755 (23/06/1946)	62755 (03/09/1949)	12/11/1958	Selby

Behind No 62755 is ex-North Eastern Railway Class J77 0-6-0T No 68392. Introduced in August 1874 as a 0-4-4T, it survived until May 1960 – 85 years, 9 months, 29 days. By contrast *The Bilsdale*, seen here at Starbeck in 1950, lasted 24 years, 3 months, 20 days. It was reported that it was stored at Whitby on 31 October 1957 along with eight other members of the class – withdrawal was to come a little over a year later. *Neville Stead 206787*

1st No	Name	Class	To Traffic	First Shed	1946 No (date)	BR No (date – w/e)	Withdrawn	Last BR Shed
230	*The Brocklesby*	D49/2	10/08/1934	Bridlington	2756 (16/06/1946)	62756 (02/07/1949)	30/04/1958	Scarborough

The Brocklesby is seen at York whilst working an express passenger service. It spent most of its BR career, from July 1951 allocated to Scarborough from where it was withdrawn in 1958. To the left of the locomotive one of the last North Eastern Railway 'Birdcage' Brake Third carriages in main line service can be seen. The last example, No E23637E was withdrawn in 1954. *Neville Stead 206792*

1st No	Name	Class	To Traffic	First Shed	1946 No (date)	BR No (date – w/e)	Withdrawn	Last BR Shed
238	*The Burton*	D49/2	17/08/1934	Bridlington	2757 (12/05/1946)	62757 (28/08/1948)	10/12/1957	Hull Botanic Gardens

The fireman has drawn the short straw at Hull Botanic Gardens during 1959 as he turns *The Burton* on the manually-operated turntable. By this time a number of the larger depots had powered – vacuum, or electric – turntables; no luxuries here where No 62757 was allocated throughout its BR career; this was one of four of the 1934-build to be withdrawn in December 1957. *Neville Stead 206794*

1st No	Name	Class	To Traffic	First Shed	1946 No (date)	BR No (date – w/e)	Withdrawn	Last BR Shed
258	*The Cattistock*	D49/2	22/08/1934	Scarborough	2758 (01/12/1946)	62758 (27/03/1948)	11/12/1957	Starbeck

This was the first locomotive to have 60,000 added to the number, actually occurring on 25 March 1948. It is seen here at Selby on 1 August 1953 at the head of an express passenger service whilst allocated to Starbeck where it arrived at in August 1948 – and stayed until withdrawal, a day after No 62757 was condemned.

1st No	Name	Class	To Traffic	First Shed	1946 No (date)	BR No (date – w/e)	Withdrawn	Last BR Shed
274	*The Craven*	D49/2	28/08/1934	Scarborough	2759 (24/11/1946)	62759 (29/01/1949)	13/01/1961	Hull Dairycoates

Of the locomotives entering service during 1934 No 62659 was the longest in service, totalling 26 years, 4 months, 16 days. It is seen here at Scarborough on 13 August 1952 during the period it was allocated to York depot. During the course of BR ownership, a total of 23 members of the class were allocated to York at various times. It was reported on 31 October 1957 that No 62759 was in store at Whitby along with eight other members of the class.

1st No	Name	Class	To Traffic	First Shed	1946 No (date)	BR No (date – w/e)	Withdrawn	Last BR Shed
279	*The Cotswold*	D49/2	03/09/1934	Scarborough	2760 (24/11/1946)	62760 (18/06/1949)	21/10/1959	Hull Dairycoates

It was reported on 30 April 1949 that the locomotive, as No 2760, was awaiting entry to Darlington works. Leaving the works on 15 June 1949 following a general overhaul it sported the first version of the BR livery with the owners name in capital letters on the tender as illustrated. It was allocated to York from November 1940 where it is seen having worked in from Leeds on 5 September 1957.

1st No	Name	Class	To Traffic	First Shed	1946 No (date)	BR No (date – w/e)	Withdrawn	Last BR Shed
353	*The Derwent*	D49/2	12/09/1934	Scarborough	2761 (03/11/1946)	62761 (28/08/1948)	06/12/1957	Selby

On 31 January 1956 No 62761 was in store in the former LMS York depot awaiting resurrection from its winter hibernation, along with two other members of the class – Nos 62702 and 62746. Allocated to Starbeck between October 1950 and July 1958 it is seen here standing on one of the through roads at Selby. *Neville Stead 206700*

1st No	Name	Class	To Traffic	First Shed	1946 No (date)	BR No (date – w/e)	Withdrawn	Last BR Shed
357	*The Fernie*	D49/2	22/09/1934	Neville Hill	2762 (24/11/1946)	62762 (10/04/1948)	13/10/1960	Scarborough

Following World War 2 the locomotive was in the wars itself having two periods in the works at Darlington – 7 September-16 October 1946 and 7 August-5 November 1948, both as a result of collision damage. It is seen here at York during the period it was allocated to Starbeck; it was used on an excursion to Wetherby Races from Bradford on Easter Monday 19 April 1954 together with Nos 62746 and 62758. It was one of nine class members stored at Whitby during the winter of 1957/58. *Neville Stead 206803*

1st No	Name	Class	To Traffic	First Shed	1946 No (date)	BR No (date – w/e)	Withdrawn	Last BR Shed
359	*The Fitzwilliam*	D49/2	28/09/1934	York	2763 (17/11/1946)	62763 (22/10/1949)	16/01/1961	Hull Dairycoates

With its buffer beam carrying all the essential information – number, home depot (York) and class designation. No 2763 is seen here before its transfer to Starbeck in February 1948, where it remained until the depot closed on 13 September 1959. Transfer to Hull Dairycoates followed for its last 16 months service until a call to Darlington resulted in its withdrawal, scrapping occurred during March 1961.

1st No	Name	Class	To Traffic	First Shed	1946 No (date)	BR No (date – w/e)	Withdrawn	Last BR Shed
361	*The Garth*	D49/2	02/10/1934	Gateshead	2764 (27/10/1946)	62764 (24/04/1948)	13/11/1958	Neville Hill

Following the conversion of *The Morpeth* in 1941 the Reidinger infinitely variable gear was reused on No 62764 in February 1949, this time using spring – not steam – controlled valves. Following testing at Rugby Testing Station – the results were not good enough to justify other conversions – it returned to normal service. No 62764 is seen on the turntable at Scarborough where it was allocated between September 1949 and July 1951, although by now it was shedded at Neville Hill.

1st No	Name	Class	To Traffic	First Shed	1946 No (date)	BR No (date – w/e)	Withdrawn	Last BR Shed
362	The Goathland	D49/2	11/10/1934	Gateshead	2765 (12/10/1946)	62765 (03/07/1948)	16/01/1961	Hull Dairycoates

The locomotive was the only member of the class to be allocated to Alston, the southern end of the branch from Haltwhistle, from May to November 1940. It is seen here at Starbeck in the summer of 1948 sporting the then current BR livery, no doubt applied at Darlington during the course of a general overhaul during June/July the same year. To the right is Class A6 4-6-2T No 9792, one of the North Eastern Railway 'Whitby Tanks', withdrawn in December 1948 it never carried its intended BR number. *Neville Stead 206808*

1st No	Name	Class	To Traffic	First Shed	1946 No (date)	BR No (date – w/e)	Withdrawn	Last BR Shed
363	*The Grafton*	D49/2	15/11/1934	Gateshead	2766 (10/11/1946)	62766 (14/08/1948)	30/09/1958	Hull Botanic Gardens

The final 25 Class D49/2 locomotives were fitted with new flush-sided 4,200 gallon tenders. This view taken at Malton shed clearly shows the vacuum brake cylinder mounted on the rear of the Group Standard tender. Of the last batch of 10 locomotives to be ordered in October 1933 – BR Nos 62766-75 – three were withdrawn at the end of the summer 1958 season. Only two D49s – Nos 62731 and 62774 – are recorded as being allocated to Malton, although both appear to have been sub-shedded at Pickering.

1st No	Name	Class	To Traffic	First Shed	1946 No (date)	BR No (date – w/e)	Withdrawn	Last BR Shed
364	*The Grove*	D49/2	19/11/1934	Gateshead	2767 (15/11/1946)	62767 (16/04/1949)	20/10/1958	Hull Botanic Gardens

Only ever allocated to one depot during its BR career – Hull Botanic Gardens – it was reported that No 62767 was in store at Bridlington in September 1957 along with three other members of the class – Nos 62703, 62710 and 62720. Carrying the 1956 crest on the tender, probably acquired during a General overhaul at Darlington between 15 March-13 April 1957, it is seen here at another seaside town, Scarborough, in 1958 a few months before withdrawal. *Neville Stead 206818*

1st No	Name	Class	To Traffic	First Shed	1946 No (date)	BR No (date – w/e)	Withdrawn	Last BR Shed
365	*The Morpeth*	D49/2	01/12/1934	Gateshead	2768 (03/11/1946)	62768 (12/08/1948)	03/11/1952	Starbeck

The Edward Thompson desire to 'simplify' Nigel Gresley's locomotives mechanically resulted in his 'back-dated' version of a modern 4-4-0 – although in this case World War 2 was partly to blame! In February 1941 No 365 was at Darlington Works awaiting parts to overhaul the Lentz rotary cam motion – Paxman, who held the licence to produce the valves, were unable to deliver and the decision was taken to rebuild the locomotive using parts readily available – it returned to traffic in August 1942 as a two-cylinder machine. Ten years later in October 1952 it was written off in a rough shunt of three stored 'Hunts' at Dragon Junction, near Starbeck – the front of the frames had to be cut away to move the locomotive to Darlington Works where it was condemned. Striped for spares the tender and boiler were reused on other members of the class. Plans to convert an additional four locomotives were cancelled by BR in August 1948. No 62768 is seen at Darlington in 1950. *Neville Stead 206816*

1st No	Name	Class	To Traffic	First Shed	1946 No (date)	BR No (date – w/e)	Withdrawn	Last BR Shed
366	*The Oakley*	D49/2	07/12/1934	Gateshead	2769 (24/10/1946)	62769 (15/05/1948)	12/09/1958	Scarborough

The platform canopy at York has clearly seen better days, following the attention of the Luftwaffe during World War 2, as No 62769 departs the station light engine having arrived with an incoming service on 22 May 1950 whilst allocated to Scarborough where it arrived in May 1948, staying until withdrawal in September 1958. It was scrapped at Darlington a matter of days later.

1st No	Name	Class	To Traffic	First Shed	1946 No (date)	BR No (date – w/e)	Withdrawn	Last BR Shed
368	*The Puckeridge*	D49/2	12/12/1934	Neville Hill	2770 (06/11/1946)	62770 (26/11/1948)	23/09/1959	York

No 62770 is seen on 15 August 1952 standing on the 'table at Scarborough where it was allocated for 11 years until June 1959 when reallocated to Selby. When that depot was closed on 13 September 1959, it was transferred to York, along with two other class members, from where it was withdrawn 10 days later. Scrapping occurred the following month at Darlington.

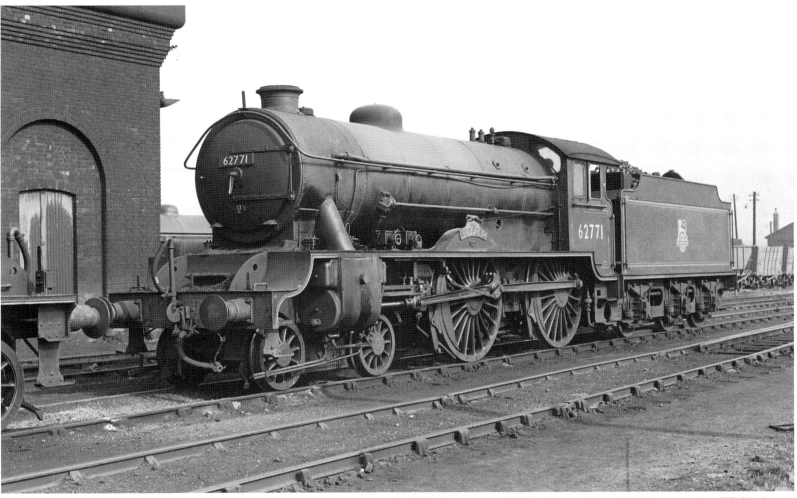

1st No	Name	Class	To Traffic	First Shed	1946 No (date)	BR No (date – w/e)	Withdrawn	Last BR Shed
370	*The Rufford*	D49/2	15/01/1935	Neville Hill	2771 (05/01/1947)	62771 (24/04/1948)	17/10/1958	York

Only two D49/2s were ever allocated to Blaydon, Newcastle, where No 62771 is seen in 1951. Both arrived in January 1949, the other was No 62747; they both left for York in June 1956. The North Eastern Railway-built depot opened in April 1900, in the form of a double roundhouse, closing to steam on 16 June 1963, demolition came in May 1966. *Neville Stead 206824*

1st No	Name	Class	To Traffic	First Shed	1946 No (date)	BR No (date – w/e)	Withdrawn	Last BR Shed
374	*The Sinnington*	D49/2	22/01/1935	Neville Hill	2772 (28/12/1946)	62772 (19/02/1949)	24/09/1958	Selby

With the water tower dominating the background No 62772 is seen on shed at Darlington on 21 May 1955, the day after leaving the works following a non-classified repair. Ex works on the 14th May it must have returned for further attention. As was common at this time, it was stored during the winter and it was reported as one of nine in store at Whitby on 31 October 1957.

1st No	Name	Class	To Traffic	First Shed	1946 No (date)	BR No (date – w/e)	Withdrawn	Last BR Shed
375	*The South Durham*	D49/2	26/01/1935	Neville Hill	2773 (10/11/1946)	62773 (25/02/1950)	05/08/1958	Neville Hill

Of the locomotives entering service in 1935, No 62773 was the shortest in service – 23 years, 6 months, 10 days – initially allocated to Neville Hill it was transferred to Starbeck in December 1947. Transferred back to Neville Hill depot in June 1957, it survived in traffic for little over a year. As usual, disposal took place at Darlington within a matter of days of it being withdrawn.

1st No	Name	Class	To Traffic	First Shed	1946 No (date)	BR No (date – w/e)	Withdrawn	Last BR Shed
376	*The Staintondale*	D49/2	02/02/1935	Neville Hill	2774 (27/10/1946)	62774 (07/08/1948)	13/11/1958	Neville Hill

Despite moving around various North Eastern Region depots, seven moves covering five sheds, the locomotive commenced its LNER career at Neville Hill depot and was withdrawn from there almost 24 years later. Transferred to Scarborough in August 1948, it spent a period from September 1948 out-stationed at Pickering that was a sub-shed of Malton. The final move occurred in June 1957 with withdrawal coming 17 months later.

1st No	Name	Class	To Traffic	First Shed	1946 No (date)	BR No (date – w/e)	Withdrawn	Last BR Shed
377	*The Tynedale*	D49/2	11/02/1935	Hull Botanic Gardens	2775 (24/11/1946)	62775 (18/09/1948)	04/12/1958	Selby

Having been withdrawn No 62775 has been moved to Broomielaw, on the Middleton-in-Teesdale line for storage, one of a number of locomotives awaiting the call to Darlington for recycling. It is seen early in 1959, scrapping occurred during May. Of the locomotives entering service in 1935 this was the longest in service – 23 years, 9 months, 23 days, although as with a number of locomotives periods were spent in store during the winter months – No 62775 was reported as being in store at Whitby depot on 31 October 1957. *Neville Stead 208050*

Want more...?

The Final Decade - The 1960s Steam Railway

Rails around Ireland

Steam Memories North East Scotland

The LMS Jubilee Class based in Scotland 1935 - 1962

Dick Riley: West from Paddington

Rails around Wycombe and the Chilterns

Find us at ttpublishing.co.uk